Tin, Pan, Cook!

by Cara Torrance

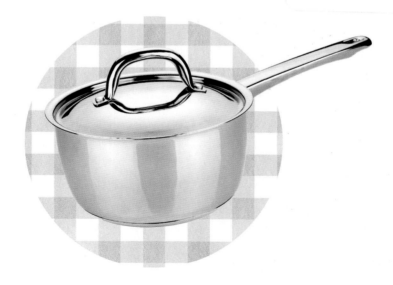

OXFORD
UNIVERSITY PRESS
AUSTRALIA & NEW ZEALAND

tin

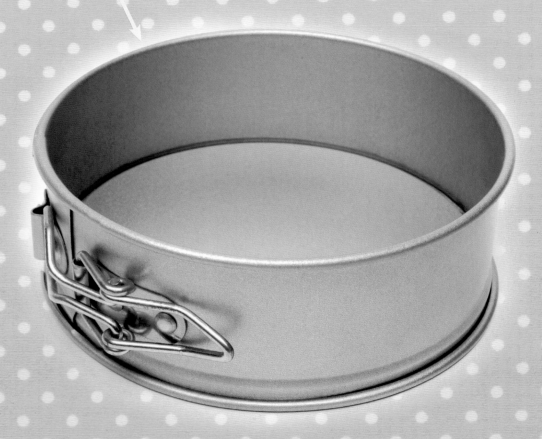

2

Dad tips it in.

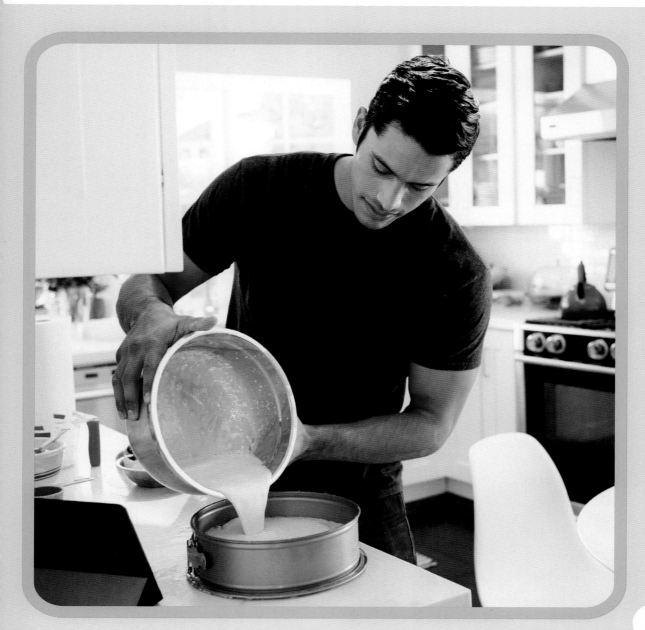

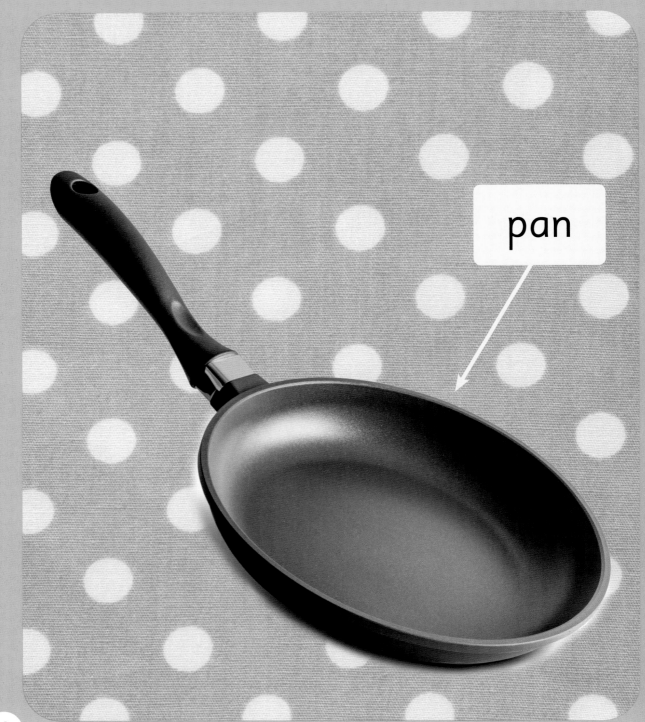

pan

4

It is in a pan.

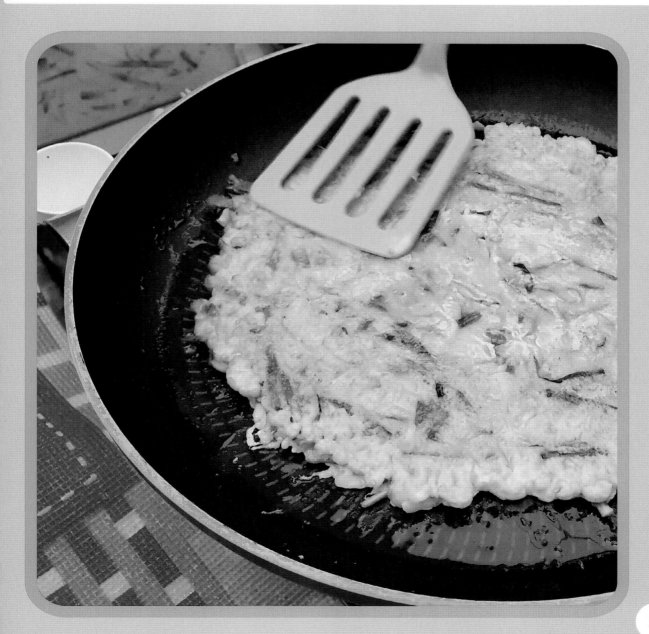

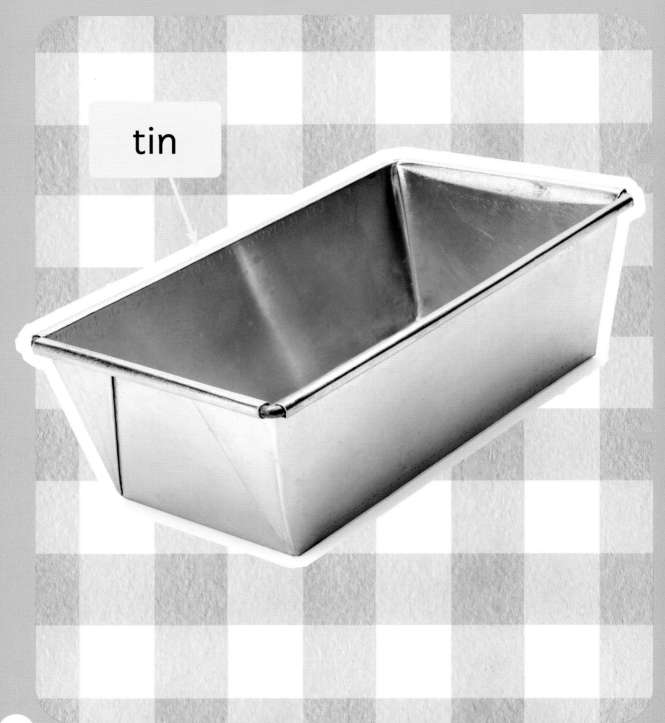

tin

It is in a tin.

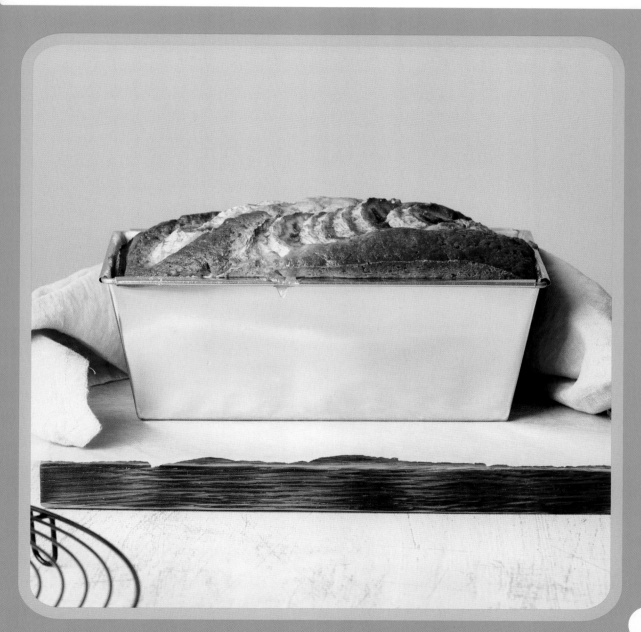

Pat it and tap it.

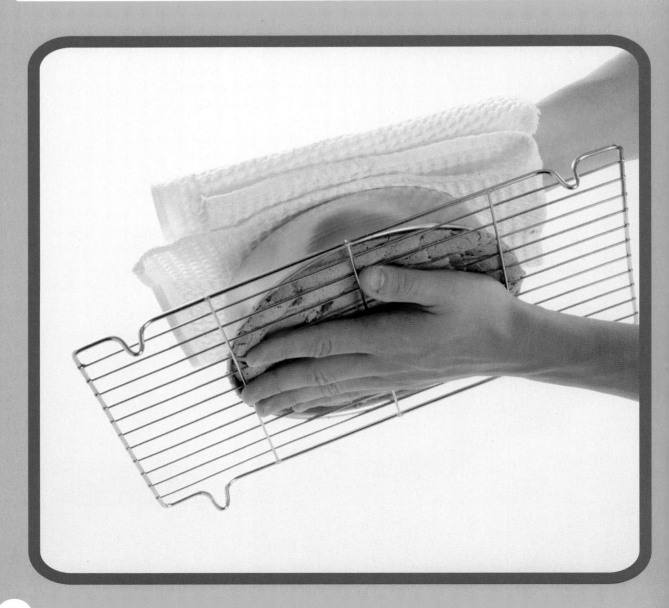

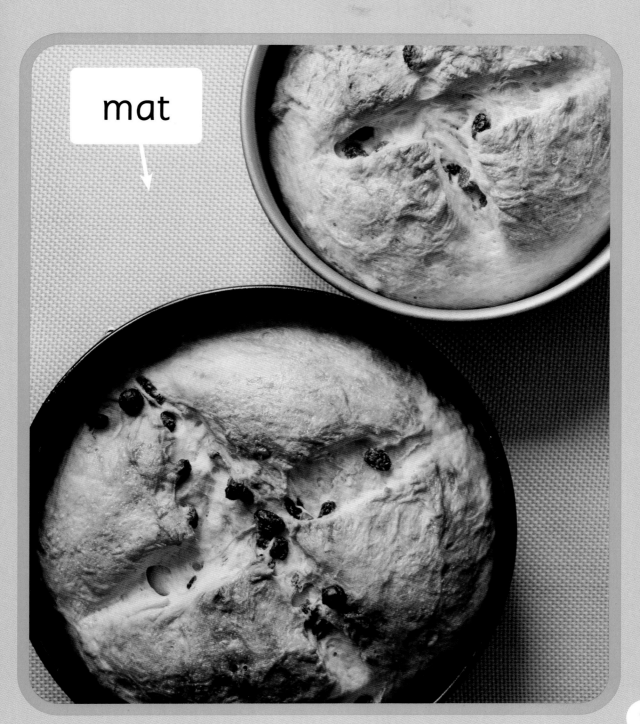

mat

Sam dips it.

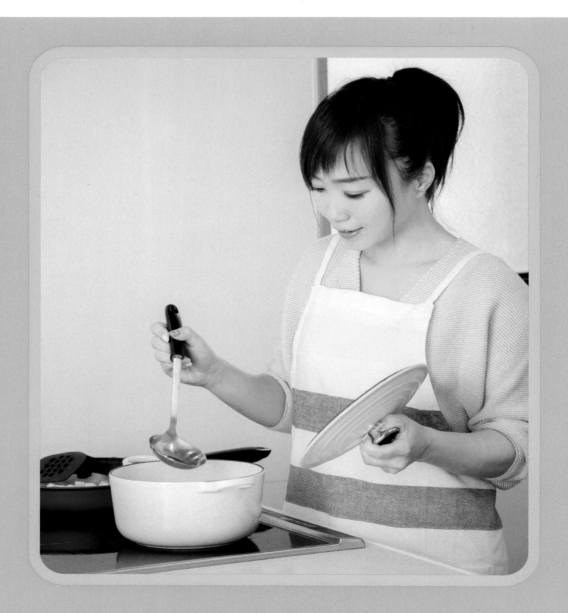

Dip it and sip it.

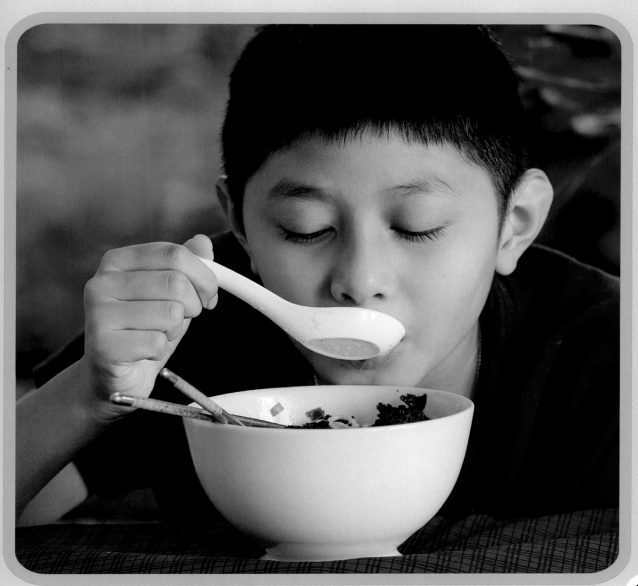

A pan and a tin.

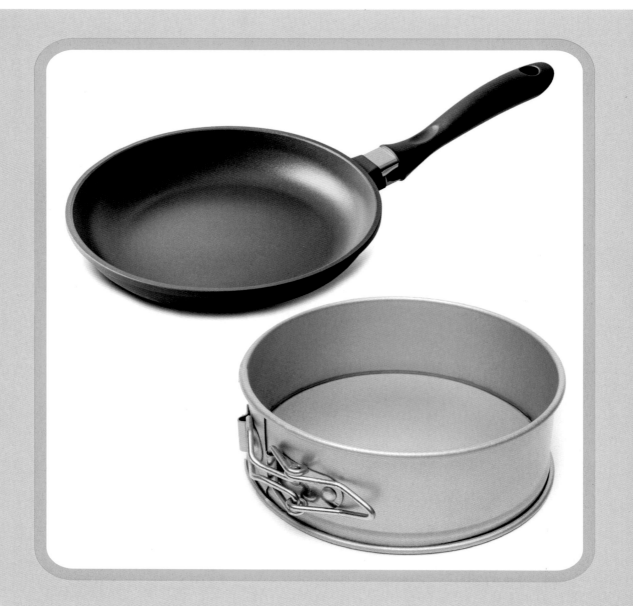